The Saints Pray for Us

The SAINTS Pray for Us

Edited by
Christina Miriam Wegendt, FSP

Introduction by
Patricia Edward Jablonski, FSP

Pauline
BOOKS & MEDIA
Boston

Nihil Obstat:
Rev. Reverend Vincent E. Daily, S.T.D.

Imprimatur:
+ Seán P. Cardinal O'Malley, O.F.M., Cap.
Archbishop of Boston
October 27, 2011

The English translation of the Litany of the Saints from *The Roman Missal* © 2010, International Commission on English in the Liturgy Corporation. All rights reserved.

Design by Mary Joseph Peterson, FSP/Photo by Mary Emmanuel Alves, FSP

Illustration credits: "Mary, the Mother of Jesus," Edwin Lebel; "Blesseds Jacinta and Francisco Marto," Mari Goering; "Blessed John Paul II," Charlie Craig; "Blessed Pier Giorgio Frassati," Don Stewart; "Blessed Teresa of Calcutta," Barbara Kiwak; "Saint André Bessette," Barbara Kiwak; "Saint Anthony of Padua," Ray Morelli; "Saint Bakhita of Sudan," Wayne Alfano; "Saint Bernadette Soubirous," Mari Goering; "Saint Catherine Labouré," Cathy Morrson; "Saint Clare of Assisi," Mary Joseph Peterson, FSP; "Saint Damien of Molokai," Anne Bergstrom; "Saint Edith Stein," Mari Goering; "Saint Elizabeth Ann Seton," Mari Goering; "Saint Faustina Kowalska," Joan Waites; "Saint Frances Xavier Cabrini," Barbara Kiwak; "Saint Francis of Assisi," Patrick Kelley; "Saint Gianna Beretta Molla," Rick Powell; "Saint Ignatius of Loyola," Patrick Kelley; "Saint Isaac Jogues," Barbara Kiwak; "Saint Joan of Arc," Ray Morelli; "Saint John Vianney," Ben Hatke; "Saint Juan Diego," Virginia Esquinaldo; "Saint Katherine Drexel," Barbara Kiwak; "Saint Martin de Porres," Wayne Alfano; "Saint Maximilian Kolbe," Karen Ritz; "Saint Paul," Dennis Auth; "Saint Pio of Pietrelcina," Karen Ritz; "Saint Teresa of Avila," Barbara Kiwak; "Saint Thérèse of Lisieux," Virginia Esquinaldo

Special thanks to the following sisters for contributing prayers to this collection: Mary Emmanuel Alves, FSP; Elizabeth Marie DeDomenico, FSP; Donna Giaimo, FSP; D. Thomas Halpin, FSP; Anne Eileen Heffernan, FSP; Mary Lea Hill, FSP; Patricia Edward Jablonski, FSP; Margaret Charles Kerry, FSP; Christine Virginia Orfeo, FSP; Virginia Helen Richards, FSP; Mary Elizabeth Tebo, FSP; Marianne Lorraine Trouvé, FSP; Susan Helen Wallace, FSP; and Christina Miriam Wegendt, FSP.

"P" and PAULINE are registered trademarks of the Daughters of St. Paul.

Published by Pauline Books & Media,
50 Saint Pauls Avenue, Boston, MA 02130-3491

Printed in the U.S.A.

SPFU VSAUSAPEOILL10-1J11-07982 7217-2

www.pauline.org

Pauline Books & Media is the publishing house of the Daughters of St. Paul, an international congregation of women religious serving the Church with the communications media.

1 2 3 4 5 6 7 8 9   16 15 14 13 12

Table of Contents

Introduction   1

Mary, the Mother of Jesus   5

Blesseds Jacinta and Francisco Marto   7

Blessed John Paul II   9

Blessed Pier Giorgio Frassati   11

Blessed Teresa of Calcutta   13

Saint André Bessette   15

Saint Anthony of Padua   17

Saint Bakhita of Sudan   19

Saint Bernadette Soubirous   21

Saint Catherine Labouré   23

Saint Clare of Assisi   25

Saint Damien of Molokai   27

Saint Edith Stein   29

Saint Elizabeth Ann Seton   31

Saint Faustina Kowalska   33

Saint Frances Xavier Cabrini   35

Saint Francis of Assisi   37

Saint Gianna Beretta Molla   39

Saint Ignatius of Loyola   41

Saint Isaac Jogues   43

Saint Joan of Arc   45

Saint John Vianney   47

Saint Juan Diego   49

Saint Katharine Drexel   51

Saint Martin de Porres   53

Saint Maximilian Kolbe   55

Saint Paul   57

Saint Pio of Pietrelcina   59

Saint Teresa of Avila   61

Saint Thérèse of Lisieux   63

Litany of the Saints   64

◪ Introduction

Friends are special. They understand us. They share our happy and sad times. They help us to become the best persons we can be.

Some very close friends of God live in heaven. We call them the saints. During their lives here on earth the saints tried their best to love God with all their mind, and heart, and soul, and to love their neighbor as themselves. They wanted to think, act, and love just as Jesus, God's Son, did. They weren't always successful, but they never gave up trying.

Every saint especially imitated one of the virtues of Jesus. Some saints became very merciful like Jesus. Others became very patient or very forgiving just as Jesus is. Still others loved and helped the poor and sick in imitation of Jesus.

Now here's some wonderful news—the saints in heaven want to be *your* friends, too! They want to lead you closer to Jesus. They want to pray to God for you in all of your needs. (We call this kind of prayer *intercession.*) The saints want to help you reach heaven, where you'll be happy with God forever.

As a Sister of the congregation of the Daughters of St. Paul, I've written and edited many stories about the lives of the saints for young people. I've learned a lot in the process. One thing I've found out is that the saints are all very different from each other. Some were quiet and shy. Others were very talkative and outgoing. Some were great leaders. Others liked to be followers. Some were young. Others were older. Some were poor. Others were rich. They came from every nation on earth. They lived in every period of history.

Reading about the saints helps us to get to know them better. We discover that every saint has a unique personality. This means that each of us can find heavenly friends with whom we feel very comfortable, just as we feel especially close to our good friends here on earth.

I have some favorite saintly friends. Besides the Blessed Mother, they include St. Paul, St. Thérèse of Lisieux, St. Bernadette, St. Faustina, and St. John Vianney. These saints show me many ways to come closer to Jesus. They teach me how to pray and how to trust in God. Best of all, they're always ready to pray for me to God. Since they are very pleasing to the Lord, he's happy to give them the graces they ask for.

In this book you will find prayers to thirty different saints. I hope that you and they will become very good friends. I hope that they will keep you always close to Jesus. I know that they will pray for you. May God bless you!

—*Sister Patricia Edward Jablonski*
Daughters of St. Paul

Mary, the Mother of Jesus

First Century, Nazareth
Solemnity of Mary, the Holy Mother
of God: January 1

Mary, my heavenly Mother, you said yes when God asked you to be Jesus's mother. What a surprise it must have been to be greeted by an angel and asked such a question! You had great faith in God. Even before Jesus was born, you loved and cared for him. As he grew up, you taught him how to love God and to love others. Watch over me, Mary, and pray for me, that I might be like Jesus. May I be filled with compassion and mercy for others and ready to help those in need around me, even when it's difficult. I know you want to watch over me, just as you cared for and watched over Jesus. Help me to remember that I can always turn to you for help, Mary. Amen.

5

Blessed Jacinta Marto

Born 1910, Aljustrel, Portugal
Died 1920, Lisbon, Portugal
Feast: February 20

Blessed Francisco Marto

Born 1908, Aljustrel, Portugal
Died 1919, Aljustrel Portugal
Feast: April 4

Blesseds Jacinta and Francisco, how wonderful it must have been to see Mary, the Mother of God! It took a lot of courage for you to be her messengers, especially when people refused to believe you.

Help me to pray for the peace that our world needs so badly. Help me to offer my own acts of love and sacrifice to make up in some small way for the sins that offend God.

You are the two youngest children ever to be considered for sainthood. Remind me that even though I'm young, my love and my efforts to be like Jesus can make a real difference in the world. Amen.

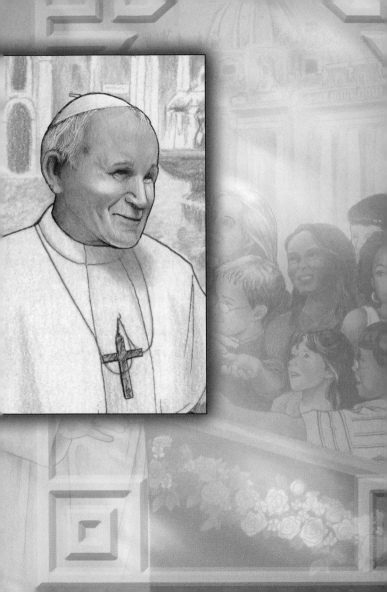

▨ Blessed John Paul II

Born 1920, Wadowice, Poland
Died 2005, Vatican City
Feast: October 22

Blessed John Paul II, you lived your life with courage and enthusiasm. Thank you for showing us how to follow Jesus during challenging times. You never let even the most difficult experiences spoil your dreams or dampen your faith.

You visited many countries, and brought the message of Jesus to our families through television, radio, and the Internet. You reminded us over and over: Do not be afraid.

Sometimes, even though I don't want to be, I am afraid. I ask you to help me to live in strong faith and unselfish love. Please ask Jesus to give me the strength I need to be and to remain his true follower. Pray that, like you, Blessed John Paul, I will always keep close to the Blessed Mother, who leads us all to Jesus. Amen.

Blessed
Pier Giorgio Frassatti

Born 1901, Turin, Italy
Died 1925, Turin, Italy
Feast: July 4

Blessed Pier, like so many young people, you enjoyed sports and being with your friends. Many of those who knew you were surprised to discover how many people in need you had helped during your lifetime. Although you were a young person, you realized you could make a difference in the lives of others. You were close to Jesus and tried to help others as Jesus did. Pray for me and for all young people that we might set out courageously on the adventure of following Jesus. May our eyes be open to the needs of others. May all young people discover the joy in loving our neighbors for the sake of Christ. Amen.

Blessed Teresa of Calcutta

Born 1910, Skopje, Macedonia
Died 1997, Calcutta (Kolkata), India
Feast: September 5

Blessed Teresa, God called you to serve the poorest of the poor, and you courageously began by helping a man you found dying in the city streets. You knew that by helping just one person, you were serving God and making a difference in the world. You saw the face of Jesus in those people who seemed forgotten by others and who were in desperate need of food, clothing, shelter, and love. Pray for me that I might be grateful for the blessings in my life and that I might be moved by the suffering of others. May I, too, see Jesus present in everyone I meet. May my heart be filled with compassion and may I treat others with love, respect, and the dignity of children of God. Amen.

13

Saint André Bessette

Born 1845, Saint-Grégoire, Quebec, Canada ▣ Died 1937, Saint-Laurent, Quebec, Canada ▣ Feast: January 6

Saint André, you had a life full of miracles. You show me that faith, kindness, and humility come from loving God, and that simple trust is more important than possessions, accomplishments, or talents. Your special love for Saint Joseph teaches me that making friends with the saints can help me be closer to God.

Saint André, you never gave up on the dream God gave you. No matter what happened, you kept praying and working for what God wanted. Show me how to trust God as you always did. I believe that he has a plan for me, just as he had a plan for you. Help me to spend my life loving God and other people just as you did, in whatever vocation I'm called to. Amen.

15

Saint Anthony of Padua

Born 1195, Lisbon, Portugal
Died 1231, Arcella, Italy
Feast: June 13

Saint Anthony, God was always first in your life. You loved God so much that you wanted everyone else to love him, too. You used your special talents for teaching and preaching to bring people closer to God and to help those who were doubtful or confused.

When things didn't work out as you had hoped or expected, Saint Anthony, you always trusted in God and in his love for you.

It's not always easy for me to put God first in my life. Saint Anthony, help me. Show me how to use my gifts to help the people around me. Help me to know and follow God's will and trust that God never stops watching over and loving me.

Pray for me, Saint Anthony. Amen.

🌀 Saint Bakhita of Sudan

Born 1869, Olgossa, Sudan
Died 1947, Schio, Italy
Feast: February 8

Saint Bakhita, suffering and sadness haunted your young life. Few people have had a more difficult life than yours. But you found your freedom and peace in the crucified Jesus, and he taught you that human pain can have value and meaning when united to him. Jesus gave you gifts of wisdom, compassion, and a great heart capable of loving and forgiving everyone—even those who treated you cruelly and enslaved you.

Saint Bakhita, you never gave in to hate or thoughts of revenge. You knew what it was like to thirst for goodness and truth, especially Eternal Truth. You teach us how to hope, how to trust, and how to keep going without ever giving up. Pray for me that I might learn to be like you. Amen.

Saint Bernadette Soubirous

Born 1844, Lourdes, France
Died 1879, Nevers, France
Feast: April 16

Saint Bernadette, God was very pleased with your humble and loving heart. He gave you the special honor of seeing the Blessed Virgin Mary many times during your lifetime. Thank you for sharing Mary's message with us: "Pray for yourselves and for people who sin against God. Change your hearts and live as Jesus taught you to. Believe that God loves you!"

Help me to put this message into practice, Saint Bernadette. Remind me to pray the Rosary as often as I can. I want to ask Mary to bring us all closer to her son Jesus. I want to be a messenger of God's love and mercy to everyone I meet. Amen.

Saint Catherine Labouré

Born 1806, Fain-lès-Moutiers, France
Died 1876, Enghien-Reuilly, France
Feast: December 31

Saint Catherine, all your life you worked hard and tried to serve God and love others in simplicity. Even when the Blessed Mother appeared to you and gave you a special mission, you were so humble that many people never guessed what you had experienced. Pray for me that I will have a truly humble heart, grateful for all that God has given me. May I, too, serve God with courage, even when it seems that no one notices.

Mary, Our Lady of the Miraculous Medal, you asked Saint Catherine to encourage people to trust in your prayers and help. Pray for me and for all those whom I love. Keep us close to Jesus. Amen.

Saint Clare of Assisi

Born 1194, Assisi, Italy
Died 1253, Assisi, Italy
Feast: August 11

Saint Clare, you loved Jesus so much that you gave your whole life to him. You chose a life of poverty, so that Jesus would be your only treasure. You wanted to spread the love of Jesus through the whole world. Even though you never left your convent, your heart was so big that you included everyone in your prayers. Your life was a light that still shines on us today.

Teach me to value the things that are really important in life: love of God and love for my family and friends. Saint Clare, you and Saint Francis were great friends. You helped each other to become holy. Teach me how to be a good friend to others, so that together we will live as Jesus wants us to. Amen.

Saint Damien of Molokai

Born 1840, Tremelo, Belgium
Died 1889, Molokai, Hawaii
Feast: May 10

Saint Damien, you learned to love others with the heart of Jesus. You saw the dignity and beauty of each person you served, where others saw only pain and misery. You embraced a new land and culture and helped people to have new hope.

Pray for me that I might see others as Jesus sees them—as my brothers and sisters. May I recognize the needs of people around me and be willing to help, even when it is difficult, just as you did. When I experience challenges or suffering, pray for me that I may always be courageous and hope-filled. And may my own heart always be filled with the love of Jesus and Mary. Amen.

✥ Saint Edith Stein

Born 1891, Breslau, Germany ▣ Died
1942, Auschwitz-Birkenau Concentration
Camp, Poland ▣ Feast: August 9

Saint Edith, you're an example to
those of us who are students. From the
day you asked for "school" as a birthday
present, to the day you graduated from
a university, you were always eager and
happy to learn. Help me to appreciate
school. Encourage me to never give up
when my studies seem difficult.

You also show me how to love the cross
of Jesus. Even when you were unjustly
made to suffer because of your Jewish
heritage, you still showed love to others.
You teach me that the cross is really a sign
of God's special love for me. When I have
a problem, or something to suffer, remind
me that God has a plan for my life and that
my suffering has value. I want to follow
Jesus as you did—no matter what. Amen.

Saint Elizabeth Ann Seton

Born 1774, New York City, New York
Died 1821, Emmittsburg, Maryland
Feast: January 4

Saint Elizabeth Ann Seton, your life took twists and turns you didn't expect. At each moment, you tried to follow Jesus. You served God by caring for your family and, later, by beginning a community of sisters who would teach others. You probably never dreamed that the work you were beginning would continue for hundreds of years after your death. Pray for me that I might be a courageous disciple of Jesus, sharing the love of God in every situation. Pray, too, for teachers and their students. May they be filled with the wisdom and understanding of the Holy Spirit and grow in their faith through all they learn and teach. Amen.

Saint Faustina Kowalska

Born 1905, Głogówiec, Poland
Died 1938, Kraków, Poland
Feast: October 5

Saint Faustina, Jesus chose you to remind us that our Savior loves and accepts us as we are. You used all your energy to carry out God's plan for you. Your day-to-day life wasn't always easy. You were sometimes misunderstood by those who failed to recognize the love of Jesus in your heart. Jesus called the kingdom of heaven a treasure and a pearl of great price. You found that kingdom and that pearl in the Lord himself.

Saint Faustina, you preached Jesus's mercy with your life, with the *Diary* you wrote, and with the painting of Jesus that you had made. You never imagined all the good that Jesus would do through you. Please teach me to love and trust in our most merciful Jesus. Amen.

Saint
Frances Xavier Cabrini

Born 1850, Sant'Angelo Lodigiano, Italy
Died 1917, Chicago, Illinois
Feast: November 13

Saint Frances Xavier Cabrini, all your life you dreamed of being a missionary and carrying the love of God to people far away. When the Holy Father asked you to journey to the United States, you generously said yes and left to care for immigrants in a new land. Pray for all those who are far from home: for those forced to leave their homes because of war or disasters or injustice, and for those who travel to new places in order to help others or to search for new opportunities. May they be welcomed in their new homes and stay close to Jesus always. Pray for me that I might be attentive to the needs of others and be a good friend to those who need my love and support. Amen.

35

Saint Francis of Assisi

Born 1182, Assisi, Italy
Died 1226, Assisi, Italy
Feast: October 4

Saint Francis, you opened your heart to Jesus, and you weren't afraid to follow where he led you.

When you decided to *really* begin living the Gospel, you ran into challenges. Your father couldn't understand you. Some of your friends laughed. To choose to live poorly and simply like Jesus wasn't what people expected you to do! But this choice made all the difference in your life. It brought you freedom, peace, and joy. It allowed you to lead many people closer to God.

I know God has a plan for my life, too, Saint Francis. Pray for me, that I might listen to him in prayer. No matter what I do in life, I want to *live* the Gospel like you did. I want to follow Jesus totally. Amen.

Saint
Gianna Beretta Molla

Born 1922, Magenta, Italy
Died 1962, Mesero, Italy
Feast: April 28

Saint Gianna, you've taught us through your example that God wants all our families to be centers of love. Remind me that the love and understanding I practice in my own family can help to make the world a better place.

You've also shown us that each person, born and unborn, is a precious and unrepeatable gift of God. Saint Gianna, ask God to bring all people to understand and believe this truth. May we do all we can to respect and protect every human life.

39

Saint Gianna, you loved life as a great gift and found holiness as a doctor, wife, and mother. Pray that I might know what God wishes me to do with my life. I want to spend it well and for the good of others, just as you did. Amen.

Saint Ignatius of Loyola

Born 1491, Loyola, Spain
Died 1556, Rome, Italy
Feast: July 31

Saint Ignatius, you loved excitement, adventures, and challenges. And you found them all when you handed your life over to God.

Once you wrote a prayer surrendering everything you had to the Lord—your freedom, your memory, your understanding, and even your will. All you asked for in return was God's love and grace.

Help me to realize that when I have God and his love, I have everything. I want to listen to God in my heart as you did. I want to say yes to whatever he asks of me. Help me to live the Gospel and to follow Jesus as closely as you did. Pray for me, Saint Ignatius. Amen.

Saint Isaac Jogues

Born 1607, Orléans, France ▣ Died
1646, Ossernenon (Auriesville, New
York) ▣ Feast: October 19 (USA);
September 26 (Canada)

Saint Isaac, your love for Jesus was so
great that you wanted all people to know
and love him too. You gave up *everything*
you had—even your life—to bring the
Good News of Jesus to the native peoples,
the First Nations of North America.

Help me to grow in love each day. Help
me to imitate Jesus and to lead others to
him just as you did. Ask God to give me the
courage I need to live my Catholic faith,
especially when I have to face problems
or things that make me suffer. I want to
believe, hope, and love as you did. Pray for
me, Saint Isaac. Amen.

43

Saint Joan of Arc

Born 1412, Domrémy, France
Died 1431, Rouen, France
Feast: May 30

Saint Joan, your life was really one of love, faith, and courage. It took so much of all three to do everything that God asked of you!

God will probably never ask me to lead an army to free my country. And I'll probably never be visited by angels or saints. But God does want me to love and obey him before anyone or anything else, just as you did.

Help me to know God's will, Saint Joan, and to do it well. Help me never to avoid doing what I know is right and pleasing to God because I'm afraid of what others will say or think of me.

Give me the courage to follow Jesus wherever he leads. Pray for me, Saint Joan. Amen.

Saint John Vianney

Born 1786, Dardilly, France
Died 1859, Ars, France
Feast: August 4

Saint John Vianney, you have shown us how to live our baptismal call to holiness through your life of selfless service.

You loved Jesus in the Eucharist and trusted in the help of our Mother, Mary, and the saints. You worked every day to help people grow closer to God, especially through the sacraments of the Eucharist and Reconciliation.

Pray for me so that I, too, can spend my life bringing the Good News of Jesus to everyone I meet. Help me to discover and understand the vocation God is calling me to. May all priests and seminarians realize what a special vocation they have received. Help them to become like Jesus.

Let me take your words to heart: "If you really love God, you will want him to be loved by the whole world." Amen.

Saint Juan Diego

Born 1474, Cuautlitlán (Mexico City, Mexico) Died 1548, México-Tenochtitlán (Mexico City, Mexico) Feast: December 9

Saint Juan Diego, you encountered the Blessed Mother—Our Lady of Guadalupe—in a very surprising way! Even though you didn't understand, you believed that miracles were possible in your life. When Mary asked you to speak to the bishop and ask that a church be built in her honor, you did as she asked. Because of your faith, the world came to know about Mary's love and care for the people of the Americas. Pray for me that I will have trust in God even when it seems difficult or even impossible. Pray for me, too, that I might always trust in Mary's motherly care and protection. Our Lady of Guadalupe, pray for us! Amen.

49

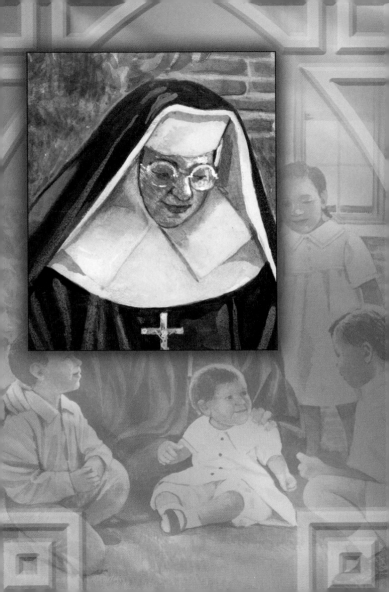

Saint Katharine Drexel

Born 1858, Philadelphia, Pennsylvania
Died 1955, Bensalem, Pennsylvania
Feast: March 3

Saint Katharine, there's so much I can learn from you. Even though many people today act as if money is the most important thing in the world, you show me that it isn't. You were wealthy but you chose to give your life to serve others. It's *people* who are more important than anything else. By caring for people of all different races, you have left me an example of how to treat all people with care, compassion, and love, just as Jesus would.

You had a special love for Jesus who gives himself to us in the Eucharist. Ask Jesus to show me how I can use the gift of my own life to make the world a better place for everyone. Thank you, Saint Katharine. Amen.

Saint Martin de Porres

Born 1579, Lima, Peru
Died 1639, Lima, Peru
Feast: November 3

Saint Martin, during your lifetime you reached out to people of all social classes and races. Your example of selfless care for the sick is an inspiration to people in our own times.

Pray for me, that I might respect all of God's creation and love all people just as you did. I want to promote peace and harmony in my family, school, and town. May the love of Jesus that burned so greatly in your heart heal the wounds of hatred and division that exist in our world today. Ask God to give me the grace to help those who are suffering or are in need. I want to see Jesus in those who are less fortunate than I am.

Pray for me, Saint Martin. Amen.

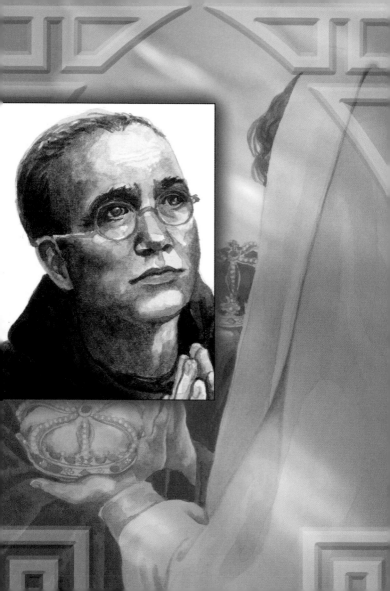

Saint Maximilian Kolbe

Born 1894, Zdunska Wola, Poland ⊡
Died 1941, Auschwitz Concentration
Camp, Poland ⊡ Feast: August 14

Saint Maximilian, thank you for your powerful example of love. You loved the Lord and his Mother Mary with all your heart. Your love made you discover new ways to bring people closer to God. It kept you peaceful and hopeful during the terrible sufferings of the concentration camp. It even gave you the courage to lay down your life for a man you didn't know.

I have many chances every day to show my love for God and my neighbor. But sometimes it's hard to love.

I know that you understand, Saint Maximilian. Remind me that Mary is always eager to help me and lead me closer to Jesus. With Jesus and Mary, I want to live and love as you did. Please pray for me. Amen.

Saint Paul

Born First Century, Tarsus, Asia Minor
Died First Century, Rome
Feast: June 29

Saint Paul, you *really* are the thirteenth apostle, specially chosen by Jesus just as the original twelve apostles were. Your meeting with the Lord on the road to Damascus changed your whole life. You became so close to Jesus that he was actually living his life again in you. This is why you could ask your friends to imitate you as you imitated Jesus. This is why you want me to imitate you, too.

I'm amazed when I think of all you went through to spread the Good News, Saint Paul. Even though you experienced persecution, dangerous journeys, and even shipwrecks, nothing could stop you from spreading the love of Jesus. Pray for me, that I might love and follow Jesus as you did. I'm counting on your help. Amen.

Saint Pio of Pietrelcina

Born 1887, Pietrelcina, Italy
Died 1968, San Giovanni Rotondo, Italy
Feast: September 23

Saint Pio, you served God faithfully
and helped many people discover God's
love for them. You were given the special
gift to share in Jesus's experience on the
cross. Many people were inspired by your
example to have hope in their own pains
and difficulties. Pray for me, that I might
love Jesus and live like him. May I share
the Good News of God's love with others.
Throughout my life, I want to give thanks
to the Father for sending Jesus his Son
to die on the cross and rise again that we
might live forever in heaven. Amen.

⛪ Saint Teresa of Avila

Born 1515, Avila, Spain
Died 1582, Alba de Tormes, Spain
Feast: October 15

Saint Teresa of Avila, when you were young, you were ordinary, like me. You wanted to be popular and have fun. But as time passed, you had the courage to open your heart to listen to the Lord. You thought about and prayed over the way he suffered and died for each of us. You wanted to thank him by the way you lived. Pray for me, that my heart might be open to listen to the Lord, too.

You became a Carmelite nun and later began a spiritual reform of the religious order you loved. Thank you for leaving your example of courage and love for Jesus for all of us to learn from. Please pray for me, that I might be as generous and courageous as you were. Amen.

61

Saint Thérèse of Lisieux

Born 1873, Alcençon, France
Died 1897, Lisieux, France
Feast: October 1

Saint Thérèse, you became a great saint and a doctor of the Church by doing ordinary things with special love for God every day. You have taught us your "little way" to become holy. You knew that nothing done with love is too small to be noticed by God. Whether you were writing or praying or playing or washing laundry, you wanted to share God's love with others. Pray for me so that I will see how much value even very ordinary actions have in God's eyes. May I have, like you, a great trust in God's love for me throughout my life. Amen.

Litany of the Saints

Lord, have mercy	**Lord, have mercy.**
Christ, have mercy	**Christ, have mercy.**
Lord, have mercy	**Lord, have mercy.**
Holy Mary, Mother of God	**pray for us.**
Saint Michael	**pray for us**
Holy angels of God	**pray for us.**
Saint John the Baptist	**pray for us.**
Saint Joseph	**pray for us.**
Saint Peter and Saint Paul	**pray for us.**
Saint Andrew	**pray for us.**
Saint John	**pray for us.**
Saint Mary Magdalene	**pray for us.**
Saint Stephen	**pray for us.**
Saint Ignatius of Antioch	**pray for us.**
Saint Lawrence	**pray for us.**
Saint Perpetua and Saint Felicity	**pray for us.**
Saint Agnes	**pray for us.**
Saint Gregory	**pray for us.**
Saint Augustine	**pray for us.**

Saint Athanasius	**pray for us.**
Saint Basil	**pray for us.**
Saint Martin	**pray for us.**
Saint Benedict	**pray for us.**
Saint Francis and Saint Dominic	**pray for us.**
Saint Francis Xavier	**pray for us.**
Saint John Vianney	**pray for us.**
Saint Catherine of Siena	**pray for us.**
Saint Teresa of Jesus	**pray for us.**
Saint Isaac Jogues	**pray for us.**
Saint Faustina Kowalska	**pray for us.**
Saint Katharine Drexel	**pray for us.**
Saint Joan of Arc	**pray for us.**
Saint Damien of Molokai	**pray for us.**
Saint Edith Stein	**pray for us.**
Saint Maximilian Kolbe	**pray for us.**
Saint Anthony of Padua	**pray for us.**
Saint Bernadette Soubirous	**pray for us.**
Saint Martin de Porres	**pray for us.**
Blesseds Jacinta and Francisco Marto	**pray for us.**
Saint Bakhita of Sudan	**pray for us.**

Saint André Bessette	**pray for us.**
Saint Juan Diego	**pray for us.**
Saint Pio of Pietrelcina	**pray for us.**
Saint Thérèse of Lisieux	**pray for us.**
Blessed Pier Giorgio Frassati	**pray for us.**
Blessed Teresa of Calcutta	**pray for us.**
Saint Frances Xavier Cabrini	**pray for us.**
Saint Elizabeth Ann Seton	**pray for us.**
Saint Clare of Assisi	**pray for us.**
Saint Catherine Labouré	**pray for us.**
Saint Gianna Beretta Molla	**pray for us.**
Saint Ignatius of Loyola	**pray for us.**
Blessed John Paul II	**pray for us.**
All holy men and women, Saints of God	**pray for us.**

Lord, be merciful	**Lord, deliver us, we pray.**
From all evil	**Lord, deliver us, we pray.**
From every sin	**Lord, deliver us, we pray.**

From everlasting death **Lord, deliver us, we pray.**

By your Incarnation　　**Lord, deliver us, we pray.**

By your Death and
　　Resurrection　　**Lord, deliver us, we pray.**

By the outpouring of
　　the Holy Spirit　　**Lord, deliver us, we pray.**

Be merciful to
　　us sinners　**Lord, we ask you, hear our prayer.**

Jesus, Son of the
　　living God　**Lord, we ask you, hear our prayer.**

Christ, hear us　　　　　**Christ, hear us.**

Christ, graciously
　　hear us.　　　**Christ, graciously hear us.**

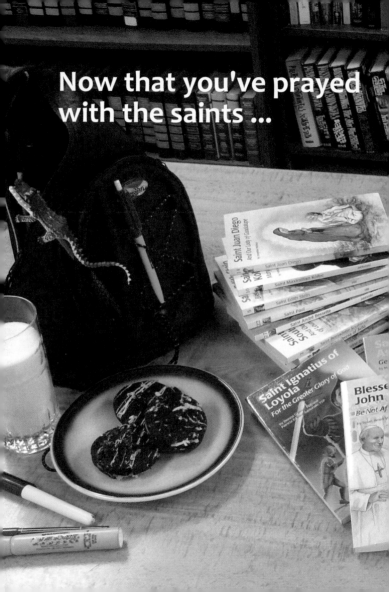

Now that you've prayed with the saints ...